The Jealousy Journeys

An Honest Look At Emotions In Open Relationships

Mona Adams

MY RELATIONSHIP BOUNDARIES
BONUS
A Relationship
Boundary Worksheet
Included In The
Paperback.

Table Of Contents

INTRODUCTION

As a child, witnessing my parents love each other made me desire that for myself; there's nothing like knowing you have a partnership of love. As I progressed into my adolescence and then adulthood, I learned I had a strong sex drive that allowed me to be passionate with a woman I loved while still having sex with someone else and having no feelings for the other person.

Despite knowing how I was, I always wanted to be monogamous and love deeply. When I recognized my wants, it was a major fight for me, and before my wife, I'd had a few short-term relationships, all of which were tough to keep monogamous, but I forced myself to do so. They all ended graciously for various reasons. I attempted to work around my "extra" emotions by suppressing them. I reside in New York City, which is full of beautiful people, and one day at an after-party for a tech conference, I was introduced to a stunning woman, and the instant I caught eye with her, I knew we were destined to be together. I felt as though no one else existed and that it was just me and her. We met again two days later on a formal date, and I brought her home after that. We never looked back.

We've recognized since then that we ARE MEANT TO BE WITH EACH OTHER. We are both in our twenties and have a strong desire to succeed. We are both entrepreneurs with a lot in common. She came up to my flat one month into our relationship. I let her in and she began to cry. She declared her greatest love for me after a few minutes of her cooling down and me forcing her to tell me what was wrong, and she continued saying that if she told me what was wrong, I would leave her and she wouldn't be able to bear it if I left her. After 30 minutes of reassuring her, she told me that, while she genuinely loved and cared about me, she wanted to have sexual experiences with other guys. She quickly stressed that it was only a physical issue, not an emotional one, as she had been with me, and that she had been battling those desires and wanted to let me know before anything occurred. I peered deep into her eyes in complete quiet, as if I could only hear our heartbeats rather than the furious honking of automobiles that you'd ordinarily hear if you lived in a NYC flat. All I could think of was how similar she was to me, but how she was honest about her thoughts and felt obligated to tell me.

She was concerned for a split second as I stared into her eyes with no response. A few seconds later, I began to cry because I understood she was just like me, craving that ONE love experience but wanting to have "just sex" with other people. I grabbed her hard and let it all out, telling her that I was the same way but that I would never act on or repress my feelings for her, but it made it so much better knowing we were alike. I don't believe in God in the traditional sense, but that day I felt linked to a deeper source that understood me and rewarded me with someone with whom I could share the sentiments I was experiencing. We married six months later and have recently had our first kid.

We still talk about that day and how it made us happier relationships and people in many facets of our lives. It may sound strange, but I believe certain individuals are built to be the way we are. In the past, many people like us would have buried our sentiments, but in this contemporary day, we have the opportunity to be who we are. We believe that the way we are has multiplied our love 100 times. The most bizarre part is that my wife is so lovely, attractive, humble, and kind that you would never believe she has a sexual side like mine.

Another thing I've seen is that many people believe open marriages don't work. I believe that everyone is unique, and in marriages or relationships where this open arrangement does not work, it is usually because one party in the relationship desired it and the other had reservations and only did it to keep the other, but eventually, jealousy or other issues crept in and the marriage did not last. But in our situation, we built our entire relationship on honesty, openness, and, most importantly, genuine love for one another, and it works for us because of that understanding. We can realize that love and sex may exist in the same individual, but that sex can also be experienced as a different feeling.

Open partnerships are a subset of consensually non-monogamous relationships. They are partnerships in which one or both parties can have sex with other people and occasionally form emotional links with them. Swinging is a type of relationship in which partners have sex with other people at parties and the interactions are solely sexual. They also differ from polyamory, in which couples can seek many committed relationships at the same time. Open relationships are sometimes regarded as a kind of medium ground between swinging and polyamory.

While swingers typically limit their outside relationships to sex with other established couples, and polyamory is all about having multiple committed, romantic partners, people in open relationships can usually have sex with others they are attracted to—with the caveat that these other relationships remain casual.

Open partnerships have a distinct set of emotional issues. While love for a primary partner is unwavering, overcoming feelings of jealousy and insecurity when outside relationships arise may be difficult. Successful open partnerships frequently rely on strong communication and emotional maturity. Partners must express their emotions honestly, address problems swiftly, and collaborate to create solutions that promote trust and understanding.

Chapter 1

THE NATURE OF JEALOUSY

Jealousy can be a particular issue in an open relationship. This is because you are more likely to be exposed to your partner's other sexual and romantic partners. Jealousy might stem from insecurity, fear of desertion, or just not feeling valued by your relationship. Jealousy is a natural feeling that we all encounter at some point in our lives. When left unchecked, it may become an issue in our relationships. Possessiveness, domineering conduct, and even violence can result from jealousy. It may also harm our relationships' trust and closeness.

In an open relationship, there are things you may do to fight jealousy. It all starts with identifying what causes your jealousy and then resolving those concerns. Communication is essential in open relationships, so be sure to discuss your wants and concerns with your partner freely and honestly.

The Psychology of Envy

To properly understand and treat envious sentiments, we must first investigate what creates them. Jealousy is frequently founded on anxieties and concerns that a person is unaware of. Fear of oversimplification, fear of inadequacy, fear of abandonment, fear of being replaced, and fear of being judged are examples of such fears. We may better control envious tendencies if we recognize what lies underlying them. We must change our perspective and see jealousy as a sign of emotional instability. This emotional uneasiness can be caused by a variety of circumstances and can be detrimental to your mental health. Recognizing our fears and why we feel envious is an important step in managing our emotions in a better manner.

When having envious sentiments, it is necessary to explain them in a non-confrontational approach. This might assist you in clarifying your sentiments or concerns and addressing any possible difficulties before they become too overwhelming. This can also contribute to a healthier and stronger bond between individuals by allowing for understanding, trust, and respect.

<u>Types Of Jealousy</u>

1. Jealousy Between Couples

As previously said, envy is more prevalent in the emotional area and love connections. In this case, relationship jealousy refers to the bad sentiments we have when we are afraid of losing our boyfriend, girlfriend, husband, or wife. While unpleasant emotions are constantly there, they do not have to be destructive. That is to say, it is normal to be fearful of losing someone because of our brains' speculations, but as long as we do not project this jealousy onto our spouse and know how to regulate it so that the relationship does not become toxic, it does not have to be destructive. Of course, you must attempt to prevent them.

2. Pathological Enmity

Pathological jealousy is common in those who have unpleasant sentiments of anxiety about losing their loved one in any situation of a romantic connection. Whether there are grounds for suspicion or not, neurotic jealousy makes the connection somewhat poisonous from the start. There can be no love when there is pathological jealousy. It is not feasible. Never feel loved enough, be punished for any interaction with another person that might endanger the relationship, develop possessive tendencies, always exhibit discontent, and try to control the partner in their behavior and way of thinking ... As we can see, pathological jealousy is detrimental and will ultimately kill the relationship.

3. Reactive Enviousness

Reactive jealousy, unlike pathological jealousy, is always there, and it arises simply because there is a valid reason to fear that the partner may end up with another person. Reactive jealousy manifests itself clearly after learning of adultery. They are, as the name implies, a reaction to something. They appear when we perceive a genuine threat. After all, the pair is always sowing seeds of uneasiness, whether they are hiding things, changing their routine, or we can tell that they are having an affair with someone. A person who does not suffer from pathological jealousy might acquire reactive jealousy in certain scenarios. That is well-founded jealousy. That is not to suggest they are all positive.

4. Occasional Envy

Occasional jealousy is unquestionably the least dangerous and destructive of all emotions. It is, as the name implies, jealousy that arises briefly and then fades away, without contaminating the connection. When a person can identify and work on their anxieties, they may maintain their natural jealousies, which do not have to develop into pathological ones. Unlike reagents, they are not caused by fears of losing the lover, but rather because the partner has changed occupations or locations, or because we are in the early phases of the relationship and are unsure whether there is exclusivity or not. They are just temporary, and if handled properly, you will rapidly return to full confidence and stability.

5. Unspoken Envy

Hidden jealousy is poisonous jealousy in which the person experiencing it does not want to indicate that he is terrified of losing his relationship at any point. To hush and, as the word implies, conceal jealousy, the person exhibits supremacy over the spouse.

It is a poisonous sort of jealousy in which they strive to make the couple feel inferior to avoid both exposing their worries and lowering the couple's self-esteem, therefore preventing them from feeling that they can be with other people. This covert envy contaminates the partnership.

6. Exaggerated Enviousness

Exaggerated envy is characterized by baseless guesses that induce us to fear losing someone. This jealousy possesses the particular attribute of the jealous individual. To excuse his conduct and feelings, he exaggerates and even fabricates incidents that never occurred, allowing envy, which has no cause to exist in reality, to be justified. They are highly harmful since they are laced with falsehoods.

7. Possessive Jealousy

Possessive jealousy is defined by the fact that it is based on possession. They are, without a doubt, the most harmful, as they may often escalate to physical and/or psychological abusePathologicallyon, the jealous individual takes enormous measures to keep his partner from having contact with others of his sexual orientation's sex.

They try not to have friends (depending on their orientation), avoid interacting with colleagues or coworkers, spend little time on social media, and receive punishments (which do not have to be physical) if they even remotely relate to someone the jealous person perceives as a threat. They are extremely poisonous.

8. Jealousy As A Child

As previously said, jealousy is more prevalent in the sentimental realm and relationships, but it is not limited to them. We have juvenile envy in this setting, which commonly develops between siblings. Young children may be envious of their sibling who receives more parental attention than they do. Given that youthful envy may develop into a terrible home environment and even difficulties amongst siblings, the father and mother must be able to notice the situation and make it clear that everyone will receive equal care, attention, and love.

9. Jealousy Projected

An extremely implausible sort of jealousy. Projective jealousy is characterized by a person who has desires to be unfaithful but projects these desires onto the partner, pretending that she is the one experiencing these feelings. That is to avoid accepting the desire to cheat on their spouse, they project the entire dilemma onto her, turning the scenario around and claiming, since they are unable to reconcile their own emotions, that she is the threat to the partnership. In the realm of psychology, this projection of sentiments, desires, and emotions onto other individuals is extensively explored. And it's not uncommon in romantic relationships. However, if mistreated, they might become hazardous.

10. Jealousy In Retrospect

Being envious of your partner's history. This is the foundation of retroactive jealousy. People who acquire this sort of envy are concerned with their partner's history, particularly what ex-boyfriends or ex-girlfriends have to say about them. Inexplicably, they reflect their partner's anguish for their love history, feeling envious of individuals who are no longer in their lives. They are generally poisonous to the relationship because the pair is angry at not being able to change their history (especially because they do not have to repent), and a fixation with ex-partners and the prospect of communication with them frequently emerges.

Chapter 2

MYTHS VERSUS REALITY IN OPEN RELATIONSHIPS

In an open relationship, the parties desire to be together yet agree to have a non-exclusive relationship. One person does not own the other in this relationship. The pair is not just seeing each other but may also date, flirt, and hook up with other people. However, unlike most normal partnerships, the parties in a genuine open relationship are completely honest with one other. As lovely as they seem, open partnerships have a poor reputation.

Here are five of the most common fallacies regarding open partnerships for individuals who don't completely comprehend the foundation of these arrangements.

1. They no longer have feelings for one another.
Most people assume that couples choose open relationships because they are no longer attracted to or have affection for one another. Open relationships are more about exploring your sexual impulses for someone

else, which may or may not diminish your attraction to your spouse.

2. They are unable to commit

True open relationships, ironically, are entirely based on trust and commitment to one another. Partners may hook up or participate in sexual activities with other individuals, but they are primarily concerned with the stability and health of their relationship. The couple talks and agrees on their expectations and boundaries in advance. This emphasizes their love for one another.

3. They are unsure of what they desire.

Being new to this type of lifestyle, it's tempting to believe that someone who is attracted to more than one person doesn't know what they want. Open relationships, on the other hand, are centered on a person getting what (or who) they desire.

4. They hit on their pals four times.

There is a widespread misconception that polyamorous persons (those in several committed relationships) are sex pals. While you may wish to have romantic or sexual connections with persons other than your spouse, others in your immediate vicinity do not become default targets. The "friend zone" exists, just as it does in traditional relationships.

5. They have a sex problem.

The biggest myth about open relationships was saved for last. It is considered that when you desire an open relationship, you are doing it because your sexual hunger is insatiable and your spouse cannot satisfy it. While persons in open partnerships may be interested in "exploring" with others, this is rarely the primary motivation for subscribing to the lifestyle in the first place.

The Advantages Of Open Relationships

1. Allow for emotional freedom

It's difficult to rely on one person to supply all of your emotional requirements, especially since their demands may differ from yours at any one time. That is frequently the primary motivator for people to want to cope with the benefits and drawbacks of an open relationship. When it comes to emotional requirements, we have a vast variety. Validation, connection, and acceptance are a few examples. These, of course, can be addressed through monogamy. Nonetheless, the benefits of having an open relationship will attract more of them.

2. Provide for all of your sexual demands

Intimacy and sex are not the same thing. Those of us who treat them the same would undoubtedly struggle with the benefits and drawbacks of an open relationship. Those who have firm boundaries between closeness and sex, on the other hand, are considerably better at compartmentalizing. This implies they are not envious when their partner has sex with another person. It's as if their partner is simply enjoying dinner or playing tennis with a buddy.

3. Establish a stronger relationship

Are open partnerships beneficial? They can be if they help you get closer to your main spouse. Imagine being able to share your innermost wishes and dreams with your lover while also acting on them. You also have the joy of meeting someone fresh in your life about whom you may openly speak. All of this communication and sharing inevitably pulls you closer together and overcomes any disadvantages of an open relationship.

4. Reasonable Expectations

There are a lot of expectations in monogamous partnerships. Working through the advantages and downsides of an open relationship, on the other hand, may be freeing. It is a situation of shared accountability with several partners.

5. Availability

Cheating causes a lot of grief in many relationships. Considering the benefits and drawbacks of an open relationship does not cure mental illnesses, but it can lead to improved communication and connection. Issues in those areas are frequently the primary motivators for adultery.

6. Additional connections

A monogamous relationship may be suffocating, particularly if you do everything together. Instead, balancing the benefits and drawbacks of an open partnership necessitates having more people in your life. You may explore and enjoy closeness with several people, just as you would with close friends.

7. Become acquainted with oneself

It takes time and effort from both parties to develop the rules that balance the positives and downsides of an open relationship. This method will teach you a lot about your wants, desires, and boundaries.

8. Improved communication

Are open partnerships beneficial? Yes, if they help you communicate honestly and freely. With the benefits and drawbacks of an open relationship, you're more inclined to communicate about yourself and your preferences. This instills trust and loyalty.

9. Lower failure risk

Some people weigh the benefits and drawbacks of an open relationship to avoid a split. After all, it's a chance to obtain some breathing room while still fulfilling your curiosity. It does not imply that you are not dedicated to your primary spouse, but rather that you want to enjoy your life. The two techniques may coexist.

10. It's entertaining.

Playfulness and enjoyment frequently keep the positives and downsides of open partnerships in balance. It's normal to be afraid of losing out and need adventure in your life, especially if both of you are open to trying open relationships.

Drawbacks Of Open Relationships

Despite the numerous advantages, there are certain drawbacks to be aware of and mitigate.

1. Fear

One of the major disadvantages of an open relationship is the emotional tornado you may encounter. If you want to keep your partner to yourself, an open relationship may cause you too much worry and stress.

2. Rivalry

If you rely more on the primary connection than your spouse, you may get envious of their other individual. This uneasiness is frequently caused by poor self-esteem and apprehension about the unknown.

3. Disease risk

One of the more concerning disadvantages of an open relationship is the danger of STDs. However, with protection and mutual faith in the regulations, this one is rather straightforward to minimize.

4. Confidentiality

It might be tempting to start lying about the other spouse if there is no firm basis of trust and limits. Suddenly, the primary connection becomes secondary, and what began as honesty becomes adultery.

5. Insane logistics

Let us not forget that coping with just one spouse might be challenging. You must handle multiple, including numerous dates and outings. Add to it the demands of your career, children, and everything else in your life, and you may be neglecting your own needs and alone time.

6. Distinctive expectations

Because both partners have different assumptions, the positives and negatives of an open relationship cannot always be balanced. If your attitudes about relationships aren't in sync, an open one might lead to misery and suffering.

7. Existential Dread

Being bombarded with inquiries about who you are and where you belong may be heartbreaking. If this is due to social rejection for being in an open relationship, you may question if it is the best thing for you.

8. Avoidance Of Stress And Anxiety

Blocking our feelings and pretending we're fine with the positives and negatives of open partnerships will only exacerbate our tension and worry. This lack of sensitivity can lead to mental health concerns and relationship failures, including perhaps your major partnership.

9. Priorities

Time management may have both positive and negative effects on open relationships. For example, you may begin to put in less time and effort in your primary relationship. Everyone expects attention, but for some couples, the prioritizing game might be too much.

10. It is pricey.

When weighing the benefits and drawbacks of an open relationship, let us not overlook the realities of life. You'll have at least twice as many birthday gifts to give. This does not cover any meals or other activities that you may have to pay for.

Chapter 3

MANAGING EMOTIONAL INTIMACY

Open partnerships have a distinct set of emotional issues. While love for a primary partner is unwavering, overcoming feelings of jealousy and insecurity when outside relationships arise may be difficult. Successful open partnerships frequently rely on strong communication and emotional maturity. Partners must express their emotions honestly, address problems swiftly, and collaborate to create solutions that promote trust and understanding.

The development of clear and mutually agreed-upon boundaries is critical to the success of open partnerships. Unlike monogamous relationships, where exclusivity is assumed, open partnerships necessitate an open discussion about the level of freedom one partner is willing to provide the other. Discussions on emotional engagement with outside partners, frequency of interaction, and whether communication about these interactions is wanted or essential are common. Setting these limits is critical to ensuring that both partners feel safe, and respected and that their expectations are aligned.

The Critics And The Appeal

The allure of open partnerships stems from their ability to give a diverse range of experiences, emotional connections, and even personal progress. Proponents claim that these agreements foster honesty, self-awareness, and a broader sense of love. Critics, on the other hand, express worries about potential emotional anguish, the likelihood of uneven emotional involvement, and the cultural cynicism that might accompany such partnerships.

The Foundation For Understanding And Trust

The cornerstone of open partnerships is open and transparent communication. Unlike monogamous relationships, where assumptions about exclusivity are frequently ignored, the success of open partnerships is inextricably linked to partners' willingness to freely discuss their views, wishes, and worries.

Sincere Communication and Expectations

Effective communication in open relationships begins with an honest and full discussion of expectations. Partners must express their objectives for taking this path as well as specify the limitations within which they are comfortable functioning. This involves open discussions about the kind of outside connections that each partner desires, the amount of emotional engagement sought, and the extent to which they intend to share their experiences.

Check-ins regularly

Check-ins become an important routine in open partnerships. Partners have continual dialogues to ensure that boundaries are maintained, comfort levels are respected, and any emergent emotions are addressed swiftly. Depending on the nature of the relationship, these talks can be planned or spontaneous, but they are critical for establishing trust and eliminating misunderstandings.

Dealing with Jealousy and Insecurity

In open partnerships, jealousy, a normal feeling in every intimate relationship, takes on a new level. Partners must recognize that envy might arise and that it should be treated as an opportunity for growth and understanding rather than a negative thing. Open discussion about these emotions aids in the identification of their underlying causes and allows partners to collaborate in developing strategies for managing and relieving them.

Reassurance and Conflict Resolution

Disagreements and disputes are unavoidable in any relationship, but they may be more complicated in open relationships. Effective communication methods, such as active listening and empathy, are critical for resolving disagreements and reinforcing partners' emotional bonds. Regularly expressing affection, reinforcing commitment, and providing reassurance become essential skills in cultivating a stable and successful relationship.

Chapter 4

COPING WITH JEALOUSY

Jealousy might arise from time to time in an open relationship (or polyamorous arrangement). While it's tempting to blame non-monogamy in this case, it's crucial to remember that jealousy is common (and good) in any relationship. Still, envy may be a terrible sensation, and, understandably, you'd want to get over it as soon as possible.

1. Respect your feelings and cope healthily.

Recognize your feelings and do something relaxing to relax. Say something like, "I'm feeling jealous right now, and that's fine." Then take a big breath and do something therapeutic for yourself. You might do some freewriting and see where your mind leads you, go for a run, or smear some crayons on a sheet of paper to express how you feel on the inside. It is very acceptable to feel envious now and again. Don't feel horrible about how you feel. It's critical not to dismiss your feelings of jealousy. Jealousy is a natural emotion in every relationship, but pretending that you aren't jealous will just make the sensation stronger.

This is good if you're feeling envious and recognize that it's a fleeting emotion. However, if you are inherently prone to jealousy, this is not a good long-term solution.

2. Distract yourself if you're obsessed over anything.

If you can't get rid of the emotion, work your way through it. Make your date with one of your other lovers, or call your closest buddy and go out for a drink. If you want to be alone, prepare a gourmet lunch or watch a movie you've been wanting to see. If you can divert your attention for a moment, the envy should subside.

If you don't have another relationship and you're a touch envious because your significant other does, now could be a good time to create that online dating profile.

3. Change your surroundings to gain a new perspective

Taking a stroll outside might drastically alter your mental state. To shake yourself out of this funk, get off your computer or phone, stand up, and move about. Dress up and go for a walk somewhere. Being outside and moving about will reduce your stress, boost your sense of well-being, and allow you some room to analyze whatever jealousy you're experiencing.

If you don't want to go for a stroll, do anything around the house to get your blood flowing. You may prepare a lavish supper, go for a walk in your yard, or clean your house.

4. Question yourself to prevent spiraling out of control.

It is frequently beneficial to punch holes in illogical impulses such as envy. If you consented to an open relationship, you might think you're crazy to be envious. Jealousy is normal, even if it isn't especially sensible and you intuitively know you shouldn't feel this way. It helps to remind yourself that your spouse is with you, and asking yourself inquisitive questions can help you recognize that. You might wonder, "Do I keep an overactive fantasy?" "Have I ever been envious for no apparent reason?"
"Am I angry, scared, or worried?" Is it conceivable that my jealousy originates from somewhere else?"

5. Take steps to increase your self-esteem.

Engaging in something you enjoy might help you get rid of this mood. Jealousy is frequently motivated by a sense that we aren't good enough. You may frequently reinforce yourself and enhance your mood by doing something you are excellent at. If you believe your spouse believes you aren't as wonderful a partner as this other person, this might be a fantastic method to remind yourself that you are a remarkable person who is valid and worthy of love.

Write a new song, get out your painting equipment, or simply sing to yourself while taking a long shower if you're a brilliant artist.

If you're athletic, you might go out with your pals and play some basketball, or you might go to the gym and try to beat a personal record.

Invite an old buddy out to dinner and talk their ear off if you're a fantastic conversationalist! Rekindle a friendship and share the joy.

6. Quit comparing yourself to your lover.

Remind yourself of what makes you distinct and exceptional. Making a list of everything that makes you unique might help you feel better. Jealousy is typically triggered when you assume someone else has something you don't, so if you're scared you're not good enough, this is a fantastic method to remind yourself that you are not replaceable. Don't be concerned about what other guys or girls have going for them since your spouse deliberately chooses to be with you.

Consider all of the praises you've ever received. Remember favorable comments about your physique, compliments about your intellect, and so on.

Examine all of the photographs you and your partner have taken together. Consider your past dates and late-night talks. Everything was tailored to you and your spouse.

Make a list of everything you do that the other person does not. You may mention how much money you have, how many years of education you have, or how many friends you have.

7. Allow yourself a small amount of healthy jealousy.

Being a bit envious is very natural and beneficial. If you're envious that your lover is seeing someone else, it shows that you care about them. Nothing is wrong with it. Couples in good, devoted, and productive marriages might experience jealousy from time to time. Take a deep breath if this isn't a frequent problem and you're only a bit uncomfortable right now since the envious emotion is so weird. This will pass, and it is not an indication that something is amiss.

Do something to occupy yourself right now, realize how you feel, and move on. Jealousy only matters if you believe it does, and it's great if you wake up tomorrow feeling completely fine.

Jealousy can be motivated by ambition—a desire to be such an excellent spouse that the other person does not need to go elsewhere. It's not bad to desire to be someone's number one.

8. Discuss your feelings with your spouse.

Regardless of why you are envious, you must discuss it as a partner. Communication is essential in a relationship, and you're not doing anything wrong by feeling the way you do. If envy is becoming an issue, discuss it with your spouse! They may be unaware that you are feeling this way, and addressing your feelings with them may provide them with the information they need to adjust their behavior and help soothe their anxieties.

"Hey, I understand you're not doing anything bad, but I've been getting envious lately," you could say. "Can we discuss it?"

Simply examine what's going on jointly from there. Discuss how each of you feels and try if you can reach an agreement. These emotions might be complicated, so don't dismiss anything.

This shouldn't be a hostile dialogue as long as you approach it with understanding and mutual respect. All you're doing is expressing a genuine emotion.

9. Deal with clear boundary infractions front on.

If your spouse violates an agreed-upon line, say something about it. It's tempting to ignore boundary violations if you suspect your spouse is doing it on purpose, but open partnerships require ground rules to function. If your spouse has violated an agreed-upon line, talk to them about it. "Hey, I'd like to talk about how sizable a moment you've been spending dating around lately," you may remark. I know we committed to spending at least 5 evenings a week together, yet you went out 4 nights last week. "Can we talk about it?" It's been really hard for me. "Can we stick to our regular schedule?"

10. If the ground rules aren't functioning, revise them.

If changing the rules would help you feel better, that's OK. The ground rules you and your partner establish in an open relationship should only be set in stone if they work. If you're experiencing jealousy frequently and it's generating conflict in your relationship, modify the rules. Changing the limits themselves to be more flexible (or more concrete) may help to lessen your emotions of envy. "I know we have a rule that we spend every Saturday together, and I keep clearing my schedule for you," you may say. You canceled twice last month, which is completely understandable, but it made me feel terrible. Should we choose a different day for each other?"

"You know how we always check in with each other when we're staying somewhere else for the night?" Is it acceptable if we change that rule such that we notify each other before 8 p.m.?

11. If you're feeling envious for the first time, look into why.

If you've never been in an open relationship, here is the place to express yourself. An open relationship differs from a monogamous relationship in its experience. For your whole life, society has told you that monogamy is "normal" and that you should be jealous if your partner is with someone else. Challenge your envy and ask yourself why you feel this way. Aim to defy whatever standards are putting you under pressure.

You're likely simply jealous because you think you're meant to be. Don't allow others to set the tone for your connections.

For many people in non-monogamous relationships, this uneasy sensation of being expected to be jealous may fade after a time.

12. Ensure that your needs are satisfied.

Jealousy may suggest that you are not obtaining what you require. You may become envious if your spouse isn't paying attention to you, giving you enough affection, or checking in on you frequently enough. If that's a part of it, check in with your spouse and tell them what you think you're missing.

"Hey, I truly want to talk about how much time you're spending away from me," you may remark. I miss you terribly, and I believe I require a bit more care. I'm not angry or anything, but it's significant to me. "Can we discuss it?"

If you don't trust your spouse to begin with, that may be the main issue here. If that's the case, addressing the reason you don't trust them is critical. Whether they're not being honest with you or you're being paranoid, addressing the underlying issue is critical.

13. Request reassurance from your partner on occasion.

More affection might serve as a beneficial reminder that you are appreciated. If you're the type of person who gets jealous easily, you might just need more reminders that your spouse loves you—which is perfectly OK. Request that your spouse be more loving or attentive, and explain that you just need more love. They shouldn't interpret it incorrectly, and this may be all you need to overcome your envy.

You may say, "I know I've been getting a little jealous lately, and it's really silly, but I just wanted to let you know that a big hug and an 'I love you' every now and then really means a lot to me."

If you are aware that you are prone to jealousy as a result of previous experiences or relationships, try to remind yourself that your present partner(s) are not your previous lovers. Every connection is unique.

14. Allow some time to pass and see if things improve.

If you're in a fresh relationship, the envy may fade on its own. It's quite natural to feel envious when you've just begun dating someone. These sentiments usually pass on their own when you understand that your spouse truly loves you and isn't going away. Wait a few weeks if the connection is new. Your jealousy may completely vanish.

If you've ever felt envious when you first started a monogamous relationship, the "open" aspect of this relationship is not a major part of how you're feeling here.

When it comes to feelings of jealousy, studies tend to imply that there isn't a significant difference between monogamous and consenting non-monogamous relationships. Don't blame the openness if it's simply "normal" jealousy.

15. Go to a couple's counselor with your partner.

There's nothing wrong with seeking assistance if you've struck a hard spot. If you and your partner(s) have attempted to resolve this on your own and it hasn't helped, there's no shame in seeking help from a psychologist or counselor. A professional will give you and your partner(s) a neutral atmosphere in which to examine your feelings while also providing you with the tools you need to overcome your jealousy. Some counselors specialize in non-monogamy, so look for someone who has already worked with someone in an open relationship.

16. If this was an experiment, end your connection.

If you tried to start a relationship and found that jealousy was an issue, it's alright to end it. If your relationship isn't working out, you do not need to keep it going. If you and your partner are experiencing some conflicting emotions, try returning to a monogamous relationship. There is no shame in it, and there is no reason why you and your spouse cannot emerge stronger than before.

It might be difficult to bring up this subject, and it can take a long time to comprehend and move through what happened. You may start by speaking up, "Hey, I understand we just started dating, and I'm not angry or anything, but I know we've both been retaining messy emotions." "Can we dialogue about changing our relationship?"

It is OK to end a relationship. Non-monogamy isn't for everyone, and if it doesn't work out, it's not a reflection of your partnership.

Increasing Your Relationship's Trust

Trust is the cornerstone that sustains a deep emotional connection in every relationship. When it comes to open relationships, this is even more important. Emotional trust helps partners to feel confident in their relationship because they know their needs and limits will be met. Without trust, the foundation dissolves, resulting in uncertainty, envy, and serious relational harm.

1. Be Consistent

Learn to keep even the smallest vows in your relationship. If you claim you'll be home at a specific hour, either arrive on time or phone to notify your spouse of the delay. Call at least thirty minutes before the scheduled time to give them notice. When you can be relied on for minor situations, your spouse will learn to rely on you for major issues as well.

2. Stay away from emotional triggers

Don't bring up topics that you know will irritate your spouse simply because you can. To establish a solid, trustworthy relationship, your spouse must know that

you will not go for the metaphorical throat every time
you disagree.

3. Interaction

It's critical to speak about big and minor concerns while
you're actively repairing trust. Keeping everything on the
table and being open about your emotions can help to
rebuild your safe relationship with one another.

4. Be realistic.

Before reacting to your lover, take a big breath. If you've
had a history of jealousy and distrust in your
relationship, it's normal to leap to unfavorable
assumptions. Before you act, pause and examine whether
any charges or suspicions are reasonable.

5. Take your time.

Building trust in your relationship will take time. You're
setting yourself up for failure if you expect substantial
improvements in a short amount of time. Accept that this
will be a lengthy road, but you and your partner will get
there together. If your relationship needs assistance, don't
be afraid to look out for couples counseling near you.

<u>CONCLUSION</u>

Emotional trust is the anchor that keeps every relationship afloat, particularly in open partnerships. Partners may handle non-monogamy with care and improve their emotional link by cultivating open communication, accepting vulnerability, respecting limits, and exercising compassion.

Individuals in open partnerships are frequently placed in circumstances that test their emotions. Partners may provide a secure environment for their partners to express their feelings without judgment or fear of rejection by cultivating emotional vulnerability. Sharing worries, doubts, and vulnerable times develops emotional trust within the partnership.

Bonus

MY RELATIONSHIP BOUNDARIES

Personal Boundaries

Date.

The reasons behind my boundaries.

1
2
3

Have I discussed these boundaries with my partner?

Yes

No

My partner's response.

Adjustments based on partners' needs.

Action Plan.

Personal Boundaries

Date.

The reasons behind my boundaries.

1
2
3

Have I discussed these boundaries with my partner?

Yes

No

My partner's response.

Adjustments based on partners' needs.

Action Plan.

MY RELATIONSHIP BOUNDARIES

Personal Boundaries

Date.

The reasons behind my boundaries.

1
2
3

Have I discussed these boundaries with my partner?

Yes

No

My partner's response.

Adjustments based on partners' needs.

Action Plan.

MY RELATIONSHIP BOUNDARIES

Personal Boundaries

Date.

The reasons behind my boundaries.

1
2
3

Have I discussed these boundaries with my partner?

Yes

No

My partner's response.

Adjustments based on partners' needs.

Action Plan.

MY RELATIONSHIP BOUNDARIES

Personal Boundaries

Date.

The reasons behind my boundaries.

1
2
3

Have I discussed these boundaries
with my partner?

Yes   **No**

My partner's response.

Adjustments based on partners' needs.

Action Plan.

MY RELATIONSHIP BOUNDARIES

Personal Boundaries

Date.

The reasons behind my boundaries.

1
2
3

Have I discussed these boundaries
with my partner?

Yes   No

My partner's response.

Adjustments based on partners' needs.

Action Plan.

MY RELATIONSHIP BOUNDARIES

Personal Boundaries

Date.

The reasons behind my boundaries.

1
2
3

Have I discussed these boundaries
with my partner?

Yes   No

My partner's response.

Adjustments based on partners' needs.

Action Plan.

MY RELATIONSHIP BOUNDARIES

Personal Boundaries

Date.

The reasons behind my boundaries.

1
2
3

Have I discussed these boundaries
with my partner?

Yes

No

My partner's response.

Adjustments based on partners' needs.

Action Plan.

MY RELATIONSHIP BOUNDARIES

Personal Boundaries

Date.

The reasons behind my boundaries.

1
2
3

Have I discussed these boundaries
with my partner?

Yes   No

My partner's response.

Adjustments based on partners' needs.

Action Plan.

MY RELATIONSHIP BOUNDARIES

Personal Boundaries

Date.

The reasons behind my boundaries.

1
2
3

Have I discussed these boundaries with my partner?

Yes

No

My partner's response.

Adjustments based on partners' needs.

Action Plan.

MY RELATIONSHIP BOUNDARIES

Personal Boundaries

Date.

The reasons behind my boundaries.

1
2
3

Have I discussed these boundaries with my partner?

Yes   **No**

My partner's response.

Adjustments based on partners' needs.

Action Plan.

MY RELATIONSHIP BOUNDARIES

Personal Boundaries

Date.

The reasons behind my boundaries.

1

2

3

Have I discussed these boundaries
with my partner?

Yes   No

My partner's response.

Adjustments based on partners' needs.

Action Plan.

MY RELATIONSHIP BOUNDARIES

Personal Boundaries

Date.

The reasons behind my boundaries.

1
2
3

Have I discussed these boundaries
with my partner?

Yes   **No**

My partner's response.

Adjustments based on partners' needs.

Action Plan.

MY RELATIONSHIP BOUNDARIES

Personal Boundaries

Date.

The reasons behind my boundaries.

1

2

3

Have I discussed these boundaries
with my partner?

Yes

No

My partner's response.

Adjustments based on partners' needs.

Action Plan.